TOUCHING ECUADOR

Also by W. H. New

Underwood Log
Night Room
Riverbook & Ocean
Stone/Rain
Raucous
Science Lessons

Touching Ecuador

Poems by

W. H. New

OOLICHAN BOOKS
LANTZVILLE, BRITISH COLUMBIA, CANADA
2006

Copyright © 2006 by W. H. New. All rights reserved. No part of this publication may be reproduced, stored in a retrieval system, or transmitted, in any form or by any means, without prior written permission of the publisher, except by a reviewer who may quote brief passages in a review to be printed in a newspaper or magazine or broadcast on radio or television; or, in the case of photocopying or other reprographic copying, a licence from ACCESS COPYRIGHT, 6 Adelaide Street East, Suite 900, Toronto, Ontario M5C 1H6.

Library and Archives Canada Cataloguing in Publication

New, W. H. (William Herbert), 1938-
Touching Ecuador / W.H. New.

Poems.
ISBN 0-88982-223-9

I. Title.

PS8577.E776T69 2006   C811'.54   C2006-900515-X

We gratefully acknowledge the support of the Canada Council for the Arts for our publishing program.

Grateful acknowledgement is also made to the BC Arts Council for their financial support.

We acknowledge the financial support of the Government of Canada through the Book Publishing Industry Development Program for our publishing activities.

Published by
Oolichan Books
P.O. Box 10, Lantzville
British Columbia, Canada
V0R 2H0

Printed in Canada

for Peggy,

for Dick, Vivian, Kieran, Pattie, and Gladys, who shared
their Ecuador enthusiasm,

in memory of Bill and Ann Messenger, Wayne Littlejohn,
and David Higgins, for the gift of friendship,

and for those who also travel with me:
who told the stories, settled the valleys, offered a home

❧

'Where your papers?' the Chief of Rostrums asked... 'Where your passaporte? What need for you to make disguise?' The Consul removed his dark glasses. Mutely..., the Chief of Gardens held out the card:... Anarquista... 'No comprendo.'... 'What for you lie?' the Chief of Rostrums repeated in a glowering voice... 'you are de espider'... The Consul shook himself free again. 'You are a spider.'
—Malcolm Lowry, *Under the Volcano*

In fact, my children, parishioners all, we make up a motley crew. We have the cheek to pursue secrets that, deep down, are nothing but the enigmas of our own lives.
—Arturo Pérez-Reverte, *The Flanders Panel*

Contents

Quito: the spider's notebook • 11

Galapagos: the castaway's calendar • 33

Cordillera: the preacher's beads/the weaver's alphabet • 47

Quito: the spider's notebook

¡Hola! the guide says as the tourists arrive on the first day, smiling. They are not travellers yet, their hands too tight on passports and *Lonely Planets*, the Spanish a signpost upside-down.

Trying to look *as if*—as if relaxed, as if they're fitting in.

¡Hola!

Their minds run backwards, over Panama, El Salvador, the Mexico they've read about, *barranca, bodega, Casino de la Selva*. Questions

> echo from somewhere else:
> *¿Le gusta esta jardín?*
> *¿Que es suyo?*
> *¡Evite que sus hijos lo destruyan!*

¡Hola! They have come south. Into the city. Close to the garden. I among them, lapsed and unfree, talking: to myself.

Quito. It is night. The plane from Houston lands at 10,000 feet. The tourists walk slowly, unused to altitude. You do not need to know their names: they are Tourists. But already a journey has begun. They are un-learning Lubbock, St. Louis, Medicine Hat, and slowly starting over, like you—like me—touching Ecuador.

> Every time you begin, the high valleys attend you, colour your breathing:
>
> Every time you clamber upward, heart racing, the mountains tender distance, invite you to see:
>
> Those roses you bought on Valentine's Day, hoping to start again, Ecuador fostered them, the cool ground:
>
> Petal by petal you rise,
> silence touching,
> filigreed as love—

The earth slopes away in volcano country. The tourists clamber. *What did she say?*

Still catching up, catching on.

They plant their feet cautiously on the black Andes, and do not know yet where to look, how to listen—*¿Que?*—what did she say?—maybe a nugget of history, a detail the guidebook's left out, a fact to take home into the rumpus room. She said

Bienvenido—adding, *Quito: the place of hummingbirds.*

> *Hummingbirds brought rainbows to the earth,*
> *say the Nahuatl,*
> *brought colour:*

So you try to imagine *Before*, in a place where history has always been, the people *from forever*. Air the colour of bone, fire the shape of stone corners, voices stilled, hidden below the pathway of the sun:

Nothing makes sense yet, Pichincha, Callambe, the mountains spilling ash and andesite into the old city. The strangulation of grey. And then *Quitolt*: the place of hummingbirds—

15

Colour: it rustles
everywhere,
which way to look first, everything is
unfamiliar, tourist

    becomes traveller
    in the slow upheaval of connecting:

touching difference as soon as familiarity: laugh, you cry;
travel, you stay at home: nowhere is without the way you see
it, words, words, corruptibility:

    Learn by seeing, the monks averred: *I turn, I look,*
    I see—how architects built llamas into the walls of
    the new church, tortoises and condors among
    the saints and gargoyled demons:

Boundaries: who knew how far the flock would stray—

Climb up, then. Look around. The weavers from Otavalo share the top of the Panicillo with Our Lady of Quito, Madonna with wings. The lady's grey in the stony light, ready to fly, to keep the babe she carries out of the devil's reach:

> What little bread there is they hold in common,
> giving thanks to the angels. The choices are clear:
> the fire, the snow: I do not belong:

The stalls of the weavers spill with scarlet, yellow, turquoise, black,

> seasons of day and dark,
> sun and blotted sun,
> the middle-of-the-earth they spin into shawl:

Some climbers buy, some turn unfed to the lady, kneel in hope, some stand, their cameras forgotten, breathless at Callambe nearby, rising higher:

Tempted—to step unprotected into the air, Liberty Square below, to soar unnoticed over the hawkers and bakers and shoe-shine boys, who go about their rituals clothed in dailiness like the sun, arrayed like night in work and ordinary wanting—

On the third day, division.

Santa Mariana still lives, the faithful vow, in the *Company of Jésus* Church. Folk wisdom says she died to stop the volcano raining ash, to stop the earthquake toppling the altar, and *therefore* lives. They come to pray, the people—though not so many as before: Pichincha's erupted again, again, and other gods intrude:

writing, for one: *teach the people to read and they stop believing,* the black robes mutter—musing here as they've done in the cloisters of cold lands, the clearings and cedar colonnades —whisper to their familiars about the *good days,*

> when images told of final stories,
> promised next instead of now,
> remembered once,
> threatened fire,
> asked to be explained—

I remember, lost in zero, locked outside in snow:

Still. Samson and Joseph stand at the Jesuit door. Some travellers read them, strength and invitation. Though few go past them, into the nave. Visitors call for facts: *when was the last quake* (eighty-seven) *how much was destroyed* (nearly all) *how much gold covers the walls* (seventy pounds, spread fine, filigree on wood and clay, like truth) *you mean like power: how much gold dropped into company coffers* (faith is numberless), the questions abrupt, the answers practised, colloquies of custom, tallies of guidebook conviction:

Mariana sleeps beneath the gilded pillars, angels looking down, apostles beckoning, demons skulking in the tropical dark: living here demands signs: Pichincha rumbles, the sun pulses, invisible workmen hammer repair—

And after division, cover: though whether camouflage or refuge remains uncertain, canopy or sheet or shade, mask or screen or shroud. No trees stand

> in front of *San Agustin*
> *y San Francisco,*
> the streets reverberate in tongues.
> Before the baroque, you are on your own:

Homero O,
> reads the hatshop sign.

> Destiny.

Step aboard. Cast straws into the windless world. Look about for temptresses, one-eyed giants, rocky shores and crew. You know how you read. *I do, I do.* You'll find whatever you're set to believe, bound for consignment, wrapped in promises of Panama and cool—

But you are learning, traveller. At latitude zero, danger comes
from the skies, ash and sunfire, wings and claws, memories

> of higher latitudes
> serpentine
> as history that's written into stone:

Chimborazo, Cotopaxi, took me by the hand—the schoolbook
rhyme still rattles through the brain, explaining nothing.
Abrading. Callambe, Cotopaxi, soar beyond the paintbox.
Civilizations, old as chaos, move like unfamiliar stars:

> Quiteños harvest the wild dogs, they say,
> clean the streets of scavengers,
> because the condors were dying,
>
> because they will die
> without fresh carcasses.
>
> Authorities
> write the bodies into the hills,
> leave them out for birds of prey:

In the narrow lanes of the Old Town, butchers once posted
red flags in their doorways on days when the meat they sold
was fresh. Now I stand on the curb opposite, watching the
traffic blur. Vans. Mopeds. Nothing. Smart women stepping over the red sill. Memory, feral as ever, the streets swept
clear:

The condors thrive:

Pumice and snow—

zero degrees:
I come from a country of zero degrees,
every winter a measure of minuses,
windchill and tuque:

Equivocal, this glimpse of *I spy with my little eye* not-nothingness: the planets freeze in the tropic sky, lovers caress in sight of the snow, the mountainsides are igneous, Cotopaxi cold:

    Dreams
    scale
    the sudden

    precipice of sleep,

    and then
    fire,
    climbing through the stars—

It is the morning of the fourth day.

Those tales of first-timers who cross the Line at sea—keelhauling, dunking: mask and mocking—circulate still among the tourists. They cruise the basket shops, trade names of liners, *princess* and *rhapsody*, chatter *Elsewhere*, norwegian spotlessness and dutch romance. At sea the round equator slips away: touch it, take it in your hand, it slides into one or another hemisphere and you are left with nothing.

But here, zero, solid, is fixed to the earth. It arcs as far as the edge of the world.

The tourist snaps pictures, moves on. The traveller

>steps lightly on the line,
>plants feet across it,
>listens to the voices in the mountain air:

Take this earth in your hand, sift clod and stone, fashion dwelling-place and field:

>*bring river into the land,* they say,
>*give balance back to the sea:*

Traveller, you hold the earth together:

>ground with your body
>the pathway of the sun—

For nothing stays.

Turn again, leave behind Our Lady of the Nine Sorrows, and this is ruin country, Rumicucho, the stone corners. *Who lived here?*

The hill is not as steep as those close at hand, though scarce air makes it seem so. Climbing, the travellers even yet are not acclimatized, to desiccated, sere:

They gasp oxygen as though it were the last, scrabble through tufts of some unlabelled, unidentifiable scrub, blue-grey amongst the stones, seeking to see:

> *Who lived here? Who lived
> Here*—

Civilizations, who once commanded north, south, invasion, valleys, power. Remnants

> sketch whatever used to be,
> before the Inca—
>
> altar, oversight.
> Walls.
>
> Basalt fractures litter the dust.
> Questions with no answers.
>
> The world is severed:

Look down: you hear children's voices, but see no children. On the valley floor, small chicken yards, small troughs of irrigation green. Farmlines spinning customary patterns, roads enumerating speed. The cloud forests hide any trees:

Look up as well. Imagine those who might have lived on even higher hills, who might have glanced without connection at those who built these walls, who might be living still amongst the clouds, their stone intact, careless of time or roads or sacrifice, or torn debris in waterless canals—

Each day adds to the day before, changes it, changes how you see. Tomorrow has already changed, without your knowing it. You go back to the Plaza Grande, it is not the same: the guide tells history, paints accretion:

> *the Bishop's Palace is also now hotel: the iron railings, notice, once adorned the Tuileries: that modern desecration on the corner made us save the rest: especially there, see, the heritage, the four-angled Inca stone in the walls of el palacio del gobierno:*

The Old City thrives on politics and habit. Liberty Square teems with tailored suits and elegant shoes: policemen slouch alert, and business captains stride: and women down from Otavalo, taciturn as postcards, pose, their babies wrapped in pattern on their backs, colour flashing from the cloth they've brought to sell: *95% mestizo here*, says the guide.

Out towards Cumbayà, the suburbs build on petrol pumps ($1.48 a gallon), warehouse the way to distance, posters for Miss Universe and football. Touching Ecuador. I listen for the sounds of Quechua, tales of the Inca that might still occupy the night, murmur shadowlands around suburban corners, whisper secrets under *arupo* leaves.

Romance.

Look again.

On a telephone line, an air plant
feeds on exhalation, particulate and grey. Grit
shapes and reshapes the boy of ten
      who polishes shoes,
the pocked priest
      who's mastered seven tongues,
spiders,
weavers,
      castaways and flies—

Stories all. Easy to find. In the guidebook, stories accumulate: they populate the mountains, track the riverbeds, assemble into everyday, cobweb, design. But listen: you do not touch Ecuador until you find room in the garden for children to play, until you tend the distance within yourself.

At Guapolo Overlook, the tourists hear of Orellana, Pizarro's cousin, *conquistadores* wrapped in romance. *There, can you see?* He rode from the Coast at Guayaquil, *into this valley*, and on through the higher Andes into Amazonia. *Lost*, the cousin thought. *Desaparecido.* Under the canopy and into tales of anaconda. *Until he surfaced*, Orellana, *singing River at the opposite ocean.*

Chimborazo, Cotopaxi, took me by the hand.

No: something

> outside
> the easy memory, the alphabets
> of precedent and protocol.

The old family story, of a distant aunt who walked from Oregon into the Amazon jungle, ready to laugh, be saved, lost, disowned. At Guapolo I imagine her like Orellana, turning the opposite way—not lost, not disappeared: already anecdote and chronicle, floating, on her own, along the great river, learning the leaves and coaxing piranha to sing—

But no escape: this, too, is Romance.

Like the promised garden at Pakakuna (Quechua, 'the hiding place'—but what is hidden here, in this gated middle-of-the-world). Light dapples the wood: *arupo* blooms white beside the hacienda. *Inti-ñan*, the sun's pathway, stripes the leaves in the orchid-hanging green.

Fecundity, not generation, bewilders. The apple orchard ripens constantly, one tree in bloom, another already harvesting: three seasons, winterless, day and night equated under the high tropic sky.

I reach out to touch reality, already disbelieving, apple in my hand.

The house serves shadow here,

> *maté de coca*,
> for altitude, *soroche:*
> peyote flourishes along the cliff,
> papyrus grows poems.
>
> Across the river the hillside dries. Ancient scrolls unroll in rails of sunlight. Words decompose.

Somewhere overhead the condors peel and peel, their eyes unrelenting—

Although the translation is still unclear. Did the people once pray to trees,

> name one of themselves every year
> to eminence
> or misrule,

or was it the Lord of the Guayacan they held in awe—

What's certain:
> the Jesuits,
> who christened the guayacan,
> called it the Tree of Life,
> tipped worship towards another wood,
> invented an Andes garden
> where Saint Peter's fish
> could swim in stone—

What's certain:
> the catalogues,
> the botanists' facts:
> *green all year,* they say,
> *with yellow flowers*
> *that last three days.*

I find a rock band, too, a guayacan recording studio, a realty company, *guayacan, best in property sales*—

The Spanish tell a different story: Ponce de León along the Rich Coast, seeking water, sending guayacan to Flanders for the dying trade: mariners who learned its properties, took it for the pox and carried it home—

Thousands, after earthquakes, gather in its shade: they kneel even now beneath the tree they call The Holy Stick, wanting innocence back, seeking out the priests who have not wandered, begging them to *impose the ash*, penitent and grave—

Touching Ecuador, you know you cannot hold: cloud forests skein the height and drift into wisp, spin out of reach, resist in peak and steepness all but aspiration:

    there? was I there?

Breathing: Ecuador

    gives you jungle, sun, love, and lets you go,
    releases you—

Where you travel after, into headwaters, plains, island

    archipelagoes,
    you've found breath to live by,

    glimpses of connection,
    leaving intact the ambiguities of liberty,

    the moon by day, darkness,
    evaporation—

Galapagos: the castaway's calendar

1

blue: the first glimpse—yellow
grass next, and then the
black: rock unforgiving as
cassock against raw flesh,
the hot day rubs salt
out of air: blade, shell

2

Encantadas: what enchantment
could the buccaneers imagine,
let alone have seen: ash erasing
every horizon, safe harbour,
promise—island after island
bleached into borderless and bone

3

black upon black, the gargoyles,
horned, marine—
the sea palpitates iguana,
Fernandina rock possesses eyes:
unblinking, the black, halting:
every step is night

4

each day different, the same,
a calendar of salt and blank
stare along the line of ocean:
narrow ledges crazed with birdlime
write vacancy, evacuation,
nest and never: never rest

5

mockingbird and mockingbird and
overhead a sudden gull:
identity is all, the tongue
coughing out names, the spit of
law: six black frigatebirds
catch the current, watch for prey

6

on the pinnacle off Bartolomé,
the red sand slicing into distance,
Melville contemplates the devil's
magic: stories, Juan
Fernández, loss and lawless i-
solation, savage Crusoe, man

7

no garden, but still a poison
apple, the juice welts the lips,
a bent leaf burns: touch is
rash, here, distance salvation—
or damn—the black-robed
frigate birds circling

8

Galápagos—old sailors say that
wicked masters turn into tortoise,
hunted, eaten, the shell become
tureen: though tortoises consume
the poison apple unperturbed,
slow giants, survivors' eyes

9

a suitable emblem, Isabela,
the black cliffs steep with overhang and
ambiguity, stirred in birds,
grey lava herons, brown
noddies, and *encantadas*: stormy
petrels, 'hummingbirds of ocean'

10

the shore, too, a growing space,
for the devil's chaplain: less desert than feared—
saltbush intoned in sloe green,
palo santo, barbed *espino*
collaring the islands grey and thorn—
do not run: go on, go by

11

go inland: the white mangrove
blocks the way only of those
who wait upon solution: go
inland, expect to stumble, wrestle
with resistance: inland pulses,
rustles with tongues, and light, and wings

12

and suddenly the black rock
is beautiful: *pahoehoe*,
lava-ribbons corrugate
the ground, pillow lava moulds it
bouldersize: balance is
everything, not *to be* but *being*

13

'pioneer plants' nudge the rock,
towards earth, mats of grey
tequilia, and in warm crevices,
abrupt as genitalia, lava
cactus: the rock has moved,
is moving, home to time

14

in the palo santo trees, even
dour Melville sees the 'peni-
tential' brown pelican—
but stillness has its own reasons:
the nest, the downy chicks, the frigate
birds unstoppable as night

15

shorelines move in tale and recon-
struction: wandering tatler, ruddy
turnstone, rearrange the islands—no
fixity here, stillness is not
the storyteller's option: the lava beds
ease east, the stones overturn

16

whatever isn't expected, can't be
planned for: *the tropical penguin*—
these rocks sport life un-
dreamed of: accept it, then,
in fragments, whole, not 'difference,'
barrenness, but contradiction

17

flightless, the cormorant here—yes, but
strong: only the air inhibits
speed—the cormorant thrives here
nesting in seaweed, adaptation:
the physics of habit (lift and drag)
slows those who only will not learn

18

—who live in bleakness, refusing hope,
or live in hope alone, without
action: the traveller who finds
prickly pear but no flower,
candelabra cactus on the lava
bed but no way to candlelight

19

Darwin did not see—dismissed
the tales of island variation
others told him, tortoise, finch—
only the dead birds in John Gould's
journals turned premise on its end:
imagine, *if only,* the blessing of eyes

20

underwater, then, inside
the sea, bless the angelfish,
its dart and day: *henceforth this day is*
Angelfish, hummingbird of
reef: colour returns, blue
fire, light, blue rain—

21

and on the surface, Sally Lightfoot
skitters scarlet across the rock where it
meets the waves—inhabits borderlands,
crabwise: Sally among the saints:
Cristóbal, Cruz, Iago, Fe,
the wandering islands—*move—move—*

22

the sea takes on a second face
after rain, un-stippled,
freed from pock and hollow:
sea lions heave, loll in a white
cove, ocean coming to rest
obligingly, on a cantled shore

23

and sea-turtle-nests, mere
indentations in bearded grit,
approximate the tideline—
against the dark ongoing, the future's
sketched in shellprint, cursive
crescents that write a way home

24

every landing site its own
promise, Punta Moreno, Punta
Suarez: so after lava, the bleak of
saltmarsh, *there*—flamingo—wings
brandish suddenness and gone,
life, all the brighter, in the grey

25

Española colours lizards—
and land iguanas, Christmas
the calendar round—red and green:
or do the lizards paint the island?
no oracles, these hooded eyes,
existing, not revealing, here

26

eco-dependence: palo santo
bursts open, a bouquet of yellow
warblers, the cordia trumpets finches:
daily their pilgrimage to the heart of
islands: the birds rewrite the air
in food, seed, generation

27

romance, relearned among
(of all possibilities)
the blue-footed boobies—*lift the
feet, flap the wings, point to the
sky*: the courting dance enchantment
(hope, impatience, comedy, delay)

28

and love perhaps, its giant wings
soaring from Chile: mating for life,
waved albatrosses turn
back to Hood, land awkwardly,
await each other meadow-tall—
arriving, not arrival, blest

29

lagoon, El Junco, the cacaotillo hills,
hidden above scalesia trees,
the matazarno: high caldera,
foggy fresh water: the way
onward a catalogue of south:
even frigate birds dip in the cool

30

in harbour, Puerto Baquerizo Moreno,
sea lions spill across
boundaries, sun aboard pangas and
anchored fishboat stern, their lives
a calendar of prepositions: *in,*
on, under, with, beside

31

touching islands, the wanderer glimpses
what it means to wander, grief and
green: every leaf a language,
feather, scale and eye, every
pebble home, the middle of the world
in a close, unending sea

Cordillera: the preacher's beads / the weaver's alphabet

THE PREACHER'S BEADS

they eat magic, the mountain people—ganja, datura—see visions i castigate as dream, hallucination: but still i feed them nothing more than bones, my words are air: the old men at the seminary argued faith is fire, but here is cold, my skeleton is earth, doubt is a marsh in which i cannot swim

THE WEAVER'S ALPHABET

standing on the plains at guayaquil, you touch the merest rim of ecuador, canals by the sea, with all of innermost yet to live,

you are not home here, pizarro's cousin: identity is only by connection yours:

the horses of dream that will drive you into high country, rafts that will carry you down amazon, these lie ahead: so dream away, amigo,

ocean at your back,

but do not expect to conquer gods or gold: only yourself is on the trail,

orellana, orellana,
1 and 1:

start close: weaving celebration
find the range of one

if i had lived here when the plated soldiers came, i would have axed the alphabets they carried, heaved the blackrobes' boxes unrepentant into chasm—if i had left already, left before disfigurement, if i had travelled inland, clambered higher still—if, if—or never learned invisibility: but i am here, lost in after, fear, lust and fingered sentences: too late i see the others changing, washing paint away along with touch and isolation

and when you go wandering through the first pass you find,

out of a craggy steep you're suddenly in foothills,
you'll think you're *there*—but watch:

the uplands settle at an inside edge, slow rumbles of aftershock: they trap strangers—chief of gardens, charlotte corday, cordelia cast to the hibernating bears:

join in, trail the undercrush: the footprints you plant on the grainy hillside will grow soon in pampas grass and hay, lines will slip aside and crushed leaves press pages into artifact—

or dare not to:

even under moonlight
there travels onwards,
the slow plates move

telling the beads, bitter: because i once believed? because believing made me live a lie? no: because i chose: it is not in us not to choose: how would i otherwise have found the hills?

for always you will find *another:*

draw him as you will, at sea or on the trail, córdoba's companion, juan fernández splitting his goatskin shoes: picture old cornelius hammering down the next-to-last spike, young *lowry, orellana,* knuckle-stained notebook under his arm,

>climbing into passwords,
>surrendering the valley ropes,
>braiding the ranges—

he is as real as you let him be: he tends llamas, elk, a forest of bighorn sheep, he farms an apple-yard, he pans for gold: in every book you know, some lowry shuttles the edge, yourself with him, keats's cortez, alex mackenzie, crossing the river panama, the great divide:

>leatherbound in cordovan,
>you read him into life, or history

they came in fog, the trinket-bearing soldiers, seamen lost in latitude and steel: they came in strings of amulets, blades on horseback, scattering ruin: they came like ghosts, like valley echoes, muffled, until too late was already here, is here, is half-heard here, in the keening

my vancouver starts somewhere behind blackout curtains,
starts in a fenced-in garden
with the canopy cloth on a wooden toy army truck,
camouflaged,

starts with a streetcar ride
and the dead soldier on cordóva street,
limp on an angel's arm,
dragged upward
beside the southeast corner
of the cpr station:

the soldier never moved:

every childhood trip to town, there he stayed, hanging:
heaven as close as maybe
the north shore mountains,
out of reach,
the coastline dissolving in war and death,
as clear as fear and rain

so i am with them—no, among them, counting beads on the mountaintop: peak and peak, distance a tumble of ice and angles: tarn and angel's trumpets, blue glass shining, moss patch, meadow: where is the messenger, list in hand, enumerating rapture? left, left, damned: i do not believe the formulas i preach, the fist of punishment, the tiers of preference and rage: why do i carry on? fear: i pack walls with me onto the mountain, afraid of daylight, letting go

the music of ice does not proceed in melody, pentatonic lines stringing angels' harps, or folk tunes traipsing the high thin air of memory—

you hear it instead in unexpected chords: raised sevenths, blues, the crack of frostflower, bloom of fissure, glacier, field —listen:

>   the strings
>   resonate,

you are part of this music,
one with the ice—

climbing, be easy: you do not need to sing
to let yourself be singing

they follow here an alphabet of season, coca, caffeine, corn, mescal: i offer a cup of wine, a wafer of words, and they ignore: PREACHER, *they say, their lips impassive, eyes alight with mocking: if i had always lived among the mountain people, i would trust the sun as they, but i am ice, i bring them ice, i mouth answers i don't believe to questions i no longer ask: nothing means to me, not even the trees*

walking the ridge, you know queen charlotte's off the edge somewhere, with adelaide and isabela: disappearing as the map returns to wilderness, their hold on borders as fixed as seafog and wine:

as you walk the ridge, distance holds empire at bay—so *here* can touch you, pitch and ice-pocket, air and blade, caress you with concentration: *now* is yours on the ridgeway,

> live *now*, the moment, flowering alpine,
> avens over timberline, columbine
> on limestone scree

if i were living with the mountain people i would seek the sunrise, cast shadows north or south across the day: I would herd llamas, court the cubs of the ridgeback bear, lie down upon the hillside, savour appletrees

think high country, early morning, california:

ice and gentian dancing the spring, claiming rock, shadow: sierra nevada, snow at the turning of the sun:

the mind's eye retrieves a climber's moment, *slip*, quick as rabbits, pica-sharp and sudden as blue:

> and breathing out,
> slowly,
> knowing life is
> focus:

only later do you realize how often bogart ventured with you, the madre lode ahead, pike and logan and unnamed scalers of green mesas touching the corners of possibility, holding on and

> holding on

if i were living with the mountain people, i would farm a plot of land, tend lambs and grow stories, children laughing through the orchard, pain and singing: if i were living in the mountains i would rise each day, my love and i as one, play skin lips hair, the body's eloquence, and whisper singing: if i were living with the mountain people i would roll love's consonants across my tongue, and linger touching in the long grass, singing

        mariners lost in storm
        on the way to gold
        or the tortoise islands—
        tierra, tierra, the cape of fire—
        rope themselves to story,
        devils riding the waves,
        mermyth howling from crag
        and broken spar:

        darwin on the *beagle*,
        measuring the breadth
        of beaks and wings,
        already imagines
        the history of the world,
        the way it is written in pearl
        and polyp, the changing
        dialect of rock:

they seek meaning, touch
the nearest end of its range,
burning with certainty—
telescope fixed on some great plan,
the story they will tell, riches
they will obtain, truth, salvation,
ale and amusement, cream
at a devon tea:

in the wheelhouse,
the captain folds his charts in four,
veers against expectation,
lives for this moment, this,
and this, embracing
likelihood, on the edge of chaos,
and choosing the freedom
of being wrong

i do not need the mountain people to know my contradictions: i live among them, the edge of something different lunging out of myth, a distant sea: being here, and never here: longing to know what the horsemen came to find, the pasture on the other side of steep: but holding back, apart, knowing destination is within

how many there are, storytellers who do not write, who hold their listeners in range and rhythm but sign in thumbprints of anonymity: goldseekers, voyageurs, plaid raftsmen singing the cordite transit of love, in volcano country:

the X in cotopaxi marks peak and contradiction, the namelessness of fire cooled in cone and hollow: not up but the edge of down, caldera, the lip of next or then or later:

mountains braid narratives, tangle syllables in myths of under, tell absolutes,

    suspended
        into sky

it is not heaven, the mountaintop, no matter how green the meadow, clear the ice: no paradise of crystals here, the soft wash of rainbow an illusion: if i were living with the mountain people i would know the wrench of work, rough palms and repetition, night abrading: i would be discontent, never suffer joy: dispute instead, arête of argument, anticline of opposition

jasper the bear used to grin his way through campsites, mountain parks, the pages of *maclean's*: no wonder i found the wild appealing, jasper trained me to trust: he had a sense of humour, knew how to laugh at the backyard convenience tourists travelled with, though that was before the fires, the careless waste:

the bears are surly now, high on corn and easy garbage:

hard to think of this as watershed, but there it is:
the balance tipped,
resentment, competition,
camper vans and loaded magazines

i am tourist here among the mountain people: i came to save, but i am castaway, pilgrim sans altar, wanderer and spy: nothing more: unless i shed the frigate bird's disguise, learn under-ice and ripple, join the mountain: can i? if i can—

    yet eagles at brackendale
    by decision, not by sudden,
    lift out of douglas and cedar,

    stir like earthquake the jet stream—

the mountains trundle under them, looking small: pinnacles and treetops point at a comicbook sky, and overhead is coloured thunder—

    eagles
    touch the unreal, upset the alphabet
    of ordinary,

    imagine ecuador

find the line: which is it? plumb, horizon, ridgeway, dash, a string of hyphens winding through the continents? cordíllera: disruption, continuity—row and ray, seed and sun, complementing water, feeding, living

my uncle called his orchard *bon accord,* the good place, in amongst the mountains: i grew sun-coloured there, happy, *of one mind* with stone and grass,

height was in reach, rocky edges roped to heaven, river tumbling out of the ice and down the world, out of distance, dancing:

i dream there still, travel continents away, back to the high valley gardens:

in dream the riverstones are smooth, laughter ripples meadowblade and birdsong,

limbs are green

among the mountain people, time gathers elongations, soft endurance: if i were with them, i would know the world by sun, the shearing stars, the thin amazing air of contemplation: i would weave a pathway through the dark, know closeness by breath, by hands

and childhood is full of mountains, reaching up, climbing into, times tables, talking down, sex, death, *i'm cliff, drop over sometime*—

the pile of cordwood that had to be chopped *before your father gets home*, and stacked so it wouldn't fall—

>   *cord*,
>   from *cuerda*, rope:
>   the wet fir measuring
>   4 by 4 by 8, knotted and never
>   easy, bark and all—

until the rhythm sets in, lift and blade honed as smooth as somersault, the slow line of firelogs rising into beauty, crag and summit, scaleable as love *if i lived above the treeline i would lie naked on the moss and lichen, stripped to the sun: stretch companionate and strong, live for noon and starlight after, one with earth and the other, lover, comet and pool: the moon would burnish me, the breezes ride their wayward course, and i would sing: nowhere is beyond reach, in the high country, undulating*

the hunter's home, the poet wrote,
down from the hill,

as though tops were unliveable, outcrop and grizzly bear unruled by chimneypot and law: maybe true—though *up* generally gets the better press (acme achievement aspiration), and *down* the blame (avalanche and plummet, low and lower hell):

does the hunter falter on his way, then, carcass on his shoulders, *barranca*-bound, do his missteps skid him?

or is something wrong, the viewpoint burdened with point of view? it is *down* that lets you see *wherever air divides, and every river pebbles into flow, writing the way back from isolation, they say an old man sits by a cave mouth, uttering wisdom: who has seen him but the jays and thieving whiskeyjacks, the condors black and gold: they do not tell, they hunt instead, put on the antic hats of industry: you cannot reach here without climbing, maybe falling, into sunrise*

under the volcano, the consul drinks his way out of the last garden, into *barranca*, fire deep inside:

>god-free, he thinks,
>omeros
>with a serpent plume—

like it or not, he's roped to past and schooled by institution: 'peter cordwainer' casts him aboard the gabriola ferry even before he knows he lives october, rocking,

>hell, hell, and
>hell, an underground of guilt,
>the memory he flies from, over the mountain,
>and can't escape,
>the suicide of friends,
>the carelessness with love

and who am i? a child of fear—no matter what i say, do not believe that those you call strong do not wear camouflage: fear churns them as it roils you: figures from the shadow past stalk us all, silverpoint and panther, men with guns and black fedoras, lists and locks and constant longing, memorized in lines

take those ropes of mountains,
cordon them by coast and prairie, narrow them,
twist, cramp, wrench, and you are

        into the panama,
        butterflies leafing in
        high jungle trees:

pacific, says the blue,

but you are nothing close,
tropic, undone, tigered by filaments of shade:

        one way, the jaguar
        strikes night out of simple sky,
        the other stabs the dark with
        uncorroborated form, lynx eyes,
        threat,
        constriction in the gorge, and running,
        just the sound of
                running

i hide my skin against temptation and the light, coil myself in rope and woollen hood, and call it praying: black is the colour of the truth i wear, judgment, insinuation—who will listen? only those in love with dying: they know me, the mountain people, leave out bowls of milk and sing enchantment against the trees

i drove to yosemite once,

smokey the bear had gone home for the night, back to the ranger station and satellite tv: he'd turned off the waterfall and turned on casino neon: you could buy beer (*cold or cooler*) and canned music, he left the elevators running, so's you'd felt you'd been somewhere, and had the postcard to prove it:

> *yo*, the guy says,
> in the pickup next to me
> at the checkout, *i can't wait
> to get to vegas,
> see the real thing*

*anxieties, like frigate birds, curve across the eye: float motionless,
stretch wingtip to the boundaryline, lashes, flat as a jailer's smile:
persistent they are, coloured starless, megrim, barred horizon*

       arête arête arête a-
       laska, interrupt and
       andes: the a's have it,
       the bony spinal cord
       of the hemisphere,
       nerve centre, motion director,
       backdrop and desert maker,

       *point and point and
       all that awe:*

somewhere after sublime and picturesque, the real:
rock and ledge
and lowry bent under the weight of popo and hood,

spiders biting the arms and ankles,
ache and getting up again,

       and angling on

if i were living with the mountain people, i would know darkness close, hear it walking, drumming the wings of birds, the raven's croak, the crack of pine spar, engelmann and lightning: i would know darkness followed me, out of distance, past fear

starting in rain forest or high mountain meadow, you don't expect desert in valleys between: okanagan, bend—and then you do: mojave, atacama,

though no zero governs here, snake abode and scorpion, prickly pear and vineyard, *vineyard,*

    oh the draught of irrigation:

lowry's keats knows all too well the lip of danger, his captain the sting of *hurucán* looping off panama: knowing how to read the storm invites it, heat solicits desert, asks in the lines of asphodel for lizard wilderness to praise *every night i dream of the soldiers winding horseback into the mountains: i am watching: every one of them is robed in black, i count them, like beads, and every one of them is me: birds go silent as they pass, the grasses wither underfoot, widows spit and orphans throw stones: brittle words catch behind my tongue and cough out useless syllables: the horses stamp on, and alphabets disperse like dust, random, coating the green*

when the K appeared on the mountainside at keremeos, cult members sold their farms, gave away whatever they could, played *follow the leader* into the hills and waited for armageddon:

most were lucky—they faded back from the alphabets of end, into past and anonymity, the sliding K just talus, the peach trees once again in bloom:

they were not alone—power drives many into madness: fire, hanging, poisoned springs, fear turning garden into ash and talk,

and stone and stone and stone and stone and stone

my shadow lies: i do not trust his sudden disappearances, his awkward gait, he tells me nothing i accept and yet i need him, seek him in the noon light and jungle dark, he fixes where i stand, cave and promontory, speaking silence: do not believe him: truth is silence: silence lies

yes, skagway's filled now with milkbars and mock saloons, and yes, the dollar rules: but you feel the undercurrent the moment you step ashore: *yukon*—not place so much as alchemy, the promise of promise, *other*, still within reach

>   across the nearest border
>   above the canal:

the white pass beckons, and i, too, take the twisting budcar up to the height of land:

yes, the random chatterers aboard find nothing in it except a fairground ride, cold creeks and the goldseekers' trails a diorama for the camera's eye:

>   but a single stunted spruce, a lake
>   where history once turned around?

in the balances of ice and wind, survival surrounds us, and in the lake a ripple writes a signature, a fragile line between then and now and limitation *you see rock, ice, grappling hook, measure height, take in the view (you like the idea of view, the nestled gentian taking root in crevices): do not overlook the fire—under the mountain it still springs artesian, desire where you least expect it, masked as apathy, inert as flint*

look up: the rockies twist like *henequen* the continent's divide, sisal, hemp, or coir—fibres of earth the earth upheaved as mountain, wound and separated, combed, knotted, spliced, roped, into cordillera, andes to saint elias—

coast and inland, old fishermen stitch nets to catch the spring run, weavers plait hats against the straw sun, cape, sarape, cedar basket, the earth their fabric, night sky the pattern of their dreaming, omineca, cascade

*i imagine seacoast now, scent of kelp and lap of tide, as once i
lived to know the hills, ragged edge and rigid sky: bound i am, by
and for, where i live, oblivion*

    lowry you old buzzard,
    tromping the woods in search of

    gin and zinfandel: it wasn't
    the wilderness you lived in

    you loved, but the
    wilderness that lived in you: set you

    circling, eye out for some sort of
    carrion happiness,

        down below,
        over and under,

        a distant *there*, blue
        roses, ultramarine:

you sent messages, in bottles,
away on the ebbing tide, imagination

flying: but bound yourself to earth—
your feet in sediment, your fingers

clenched, your eyes
lowered, away from the hills

that line of horses snaking through the passes: if i lived among the mountain people, high above the anaconda valleys, safe except from snow, i would eye them as the cats do, slitting light into hunger, satisfaction: the horses, roped in sequence, trudge without emotion: they do not know they stumble over time

home is the mountains, the mountains
are home:

    that far ruggedness,
    the line of purple looming
    the cloud forest
    dances with,
    obscures—

    or close, those cornices of invitation,
    come see, they say, *come*
    see what happens here—
    cave and hollow, flute and ledge and
    col—

everywhere the names of claim, catalogues of mere slope and valley, rivercourse and fall, and cairns of space: nest, cabin, thicket, aerie, pond:

    beyond them tumbles resonance,
    the way the heart moves,
    knowing connection,
    the way the mountains, cordate,
    circle home

if i were living then among the mountain people, i would watch the soldiers trample through, discovering: i would stand aside, watch them startle the earth with horses, lift south and east from compasses and nail direction into the sun—the scree i hid in, terraces i lay upon, grassy slopes i thought would never end, would end—if i were mountain i would know already that the earth moves, rumble incautious into narrowness and till, balk passage, rock the underfoot, watch the interlopers stagger: fire, limbs would melt: air, the lungs collapse: advance, withdraw, intent and blind: if i were later i would rail against widowhood, the gods, inaction: but i am ice, i am ice, i would be rain

the continents speak in this mountain corduroy, the heart beating beneath its ribs:

you, i, walkers,
we, too, speak through a tussle of bones, touch earth and breathe sky, aspiring:

the reach of arm and ridgeway spells out lines that join, tie us, embrace across recorded borders, write walking rhythms through space into *listen*

for reading north depends on south, and south, north: the idea of here discovers there,

    condors above,
    fire below—

touches,
moves on—

    and there ...

i hear *north* in the ice-blue crisp of winter mountains, pine and spruce-needles on the forest floor—while *south* sways palms—

until south's south becomes *north*, and north the palm country:

the skies reverse then, cross and cassiopeia, lines enclosed in sphere—

read as i will, toss the alphabet of days, chase calendars into distance, north lives within me, i in north, aboard *here*, the moving continents, chords joining arc's ends, singing, and starting again, travelling the music of how we listen,

    cordilléra,

how the heart beats,

    how we see

Acknowledgments

With thanks to many friends: Laurie, Jack, Hiro, Ron, and Pat, for laughter, keen eyes, and endless encouragement. Thanks also to my Erickson cousins, for sharing their mountains; to George and Inge, for sharing other paths; and to Florencia and the group of seven travellers in Ecuador, for companionship on a journey.

A short, early version of 'Quito' (beginning 'earth gives up its history here') was first published in *For George*, a tribute to George McWhirter, on his retirement in 2004.

Touching Ecuador alludes occasionally to works by several other writers, from Shakespeare, Keats, and Robert Louis Stevenson to Homer, Lawrence, Dante, Donne, and the Psalms. 'Romance' (*Chimborazo, Cotopaxi, took me by the hand*), by the Australian-born Walter J. Turner, has long been a staple of elementary school textbooks. Herman Melville's *The Encantadas* gave rise to several phrases in 'Galapagos,' as did Charles Darwin's brief comments on finches and tortoises in *The Voyage of the 'Beagle'*; Darwin developed his influential theories about adaptation much further in his subsequent writings, after (in part) he had acknowledged the observations of John Gould. 'Cordillera' and 'Quito' allude to several Malcolm Lowry titles, from 'Gin and Goldenrod' and 'Through the Panama' to *Ultramarine* and *Under the Volcano*. Lowry's character Geoffrey Firmin, the infirm Consul in *Under the Volcano* (which opens in Mexico, in a place called the Casino de la Selva), mistranslates the questions that begin with '*¿Le gusta esta jardín . . . ?*' The story of another Lowry character, Peter Cordwainer ('ropemaker'), informs a suicide narrative in the posthumously published *October Ferry to Gabriola*. But the 'lowry' figure in 'Cordillera' is a fiction.

W.H. New likes to travel, and recently has enjoyed trips to Winnipeg in mid-winter, Trigance in spring, and Quito, where all seasons are one. He has written three books for children, and edited the *Encyclopedia of Literature in Canada*, among other books. *Touching Ecuador* is his seventh book of poems. His most recent book, *Underwood Log*, was shortlisted for the 2005 Governor General's Literary Award for Poetry. W.H. New is the recipient of the Lorne Pierce Medal for his contributions to imaginative and critical literature, and also of the 2004 Governor General's International Award in Canadian Studies.